Book title

Facebook Votes For Online Success

Author

Nauman Ashraf

Note

Ebooks on Smashwords

https://www.smashwords.com/books/view/549782?ref=nauman098

Ebooks on Amazon

http://amzn.to/1KkR6pW

Facebook votes for online success

Contents

Introduction

Facebook votes are helpful for increasing the worth of any type of contest. There are many types of contests on internet which are launched from time to time. Facebook is hosting many types of contests for users.

Facebook votes are given to contests on facebook so that users could show the engagement. Free and paid modes are available for increasing Facebook votes for contests. You can use these methods for your contests on facebook and get a lot of engagement in the form of Facebook votes which will also help in online success.

Professionals for increasing Facebook votes

Facebook votes are posted for contests in facebook. There are many professionals through which any person is able to increase Facebook votes. When you have launched a contest in facebook then you must use professional services so that you could increase Facebook votes.

Contests with many facebook votes are able to get more attention and engagement from users. People are in search of good contests on facebook. More Facebook votes are criteria which are used by users of facebook in determination of quality of contests.

If a contest has many Facebook votes then it is thought to be good as compared with a contest which is having reduced number of Facebook votes. You can invest some money in order to have many Facebook votes in the start.

When you have obtained Facebook votes for your new contests then the process will continue and many more Facebook votes will follow. You can also send messages to your followers on facebook so that they can check your contests and cast Facebook votes for you. You can also join many communities for free on facebook and post links for your contests by requesting to get Facebook votes.

Many people from the communities on facebook are ready to cast Facebook votes on request of others. However these free methods are not going to give you guaranteed results. In order to get guaranteed results in the form of increase in Facebook votes to a certain limit you must invest some money.

There are many types of packages from professionals through which you can make selection for getting desired number of Facebook votes. You can check different modes of payment through internet for getting Facebook votes.

When you have invested some money for getting Facebook votes then you are on your way for getting more online exposure. Many votes for your contest means, that it is liked and engaging to people. With an increase in the number of Facebook votes you are also having more chances of getting traffic from other sites.

Search engines will show your contests with many Facebook votes on top of search results for people who are looking for related topics. This is good for getting more traffic to your contests and increasing the number of Facebook votes.

Professionals are giving time limits in which you will get all the Facebook votes for your contests. These services are performed by using unique IP addresses which are giving Facebook votes in the set time period.

All the Facebook votes would be unique and you will be able to add value to your contests. Many real Facebook votes will follow once you have many votes through professionals in this field. It is hard to increase v without making any investment.

You have to ask many people on facebook and share your contests with them so that they can check and cast Facebook votes. By making some investment for purchasing Facebook votes you are able to complete the process sooner and easier. Satisfaction of users is guaranteed by professionals who are providing services related with increasing Facebook votes for contests on facebook.

Paid modes of getting Facebook votes

Many professionals are available through which Facebook votes could be purchased on payment of some price. If you have a contest on facebook then you can pay some money to professionals so that more votes could be obtained.

There are many benefits of getting Facebook votes through professionals. These votes will be attracting real humans so that they can cast their votes. When your contest will be getting many votes then more and more people will join the contest by thinking that it is important therefore it is getting more votes.

This will increase the worth of your contest and you will get more votes. This process will continue till you will get the targeted number of votes and even more. This process can be started by investing some money for getting votes.

When you have invested some money for getting Facebook votes then you are able to see the process of getting more votes will become automatic. You can compare different sites for choosing the best packages in order to get Facebook votes. Some search on internet is helpful in making selection of the desired packages which will increase many Facebook votes in your set time period.

Professionals have many profiles and programs which are managing these profiles. You will get Facebook votes from unique users in small time period. This will be checked by you and you will be able to see the increase automatically after the professional services are obtained for increasing Facebook votes.

There are many exchanges which are working on a credit system. You can pay some amount in order to purchase set amount of credits on these exchanges. These credits are used for getting votes on your contests. These Facebook votes are going to be increased at a fast rate as many people are using such exchanges.

These social exchanges are working well and users are able to allocate the credits to the desired number of contests for getting Facebook votes. Exact number of votes could be purchased and used through sites which are available on internet.

This is helpful in increasing the popularity of your contests and highlights them to many users of facebook. In start it is hard to attract voters for your contests as the contest is new. You can use paid services for getting Facebook votes for your contests in start and then you will notice that many real votes are coming to your contests.

This process is working well for all types of contests and you are not required to have many friends and request them for casting Facebook votes. If you have some friends in facebook even then you can use paid modes for getting many Facebook votes. This is automatic process which is working for contests and increasing their worth.

Many people are using facebook in routine life therefore it is good to have many Facebook votes for contests. This is a good form of advertisement which is giving instant results in the form of more traffic on your main site and increasing the chances of dealings and profits.

Marketing through Facebook votes

Facebook votes can be used for marketing purposes. If you have a contest on facebook then you must try to get many Facebook votes so that you can use your contest for marketing. It is important to use different methods in order to have more Facebook votes for your contest.

You can use many methods in start so that the process could be improved and more Facebook votes could be received by your contests on facebook. You must choose specific terms on your contest page so that people could participate and use links for getting traffic.

Professional ways of asking questions in contests on facebook are liked by users. More Facebook votes could be obtained if the contests are of a high quality. You can see many contests on facebook which have different number of votes.

These Facebook votes are obtained through different ways and you can also use these ways for increasing the number of Facebook votes for your contests. Proper placement of items is important on contests so that the traffic could give Facebook votes and also engage in the contests. When you are working seriously on your contests on facebook then you will get Facebook votes which will increase their worth.

Some investment could be used for increasing Facebook votes for your contests in start. There are many professionals who are providing services for increasing Facebook votes for contests. You can compare offers from these professionals in order to have the best selection.

With a good selection you are able to get instant results in the form of more Facebook votes for your contests. Search engines like those contests on facebook which have many Facebook votes and show them on top of searches when a person is looking for related terms. This is giving traffic and marketing opportunities through search engines.

Facebook is a famous social site and any contest which is famous on facebook is going to get more exposure on search engines. You can see many types of facebook pages which are shown as a result of searches. Those pages are not simple as they have many Facebook votes in different forms.

If you are willing to use your contest for marketing purposes on facebook then make sure that you are using Facebook votes for increasing the speed of this process. This process will give instant results in the form of more traffic and more marketing in the online world. If your contest is famous then you will get traffic from facebook and also from search engines.

You can ask your friends in order to cast their votes for your contests in order to increase Facebook votes. Many communities are available on facebook in which you can post requests about your contests so that more Facebook votes could be obtained.

You can invest some money in online sites which are managed by professionals. These professionals are giving Facebook votes for any type of contests so that the users could take a good start in marketing through their contests. Any method could be used for increasing Facebook votes for contests so that it could be used for marketing purposes.

Importance of Facebook votes

Facebook votes are important for users as these are giving indication that the contest is very important. Those contests on facebook which have reduced number of Facebook votes are thought to be less popular and many people are not using them and casting their votes on them.

Those contests on facebook which are having many Facebook votes are liked by other users of facebook and they continue to use them and participate in them. More Facebook votes on any contest are also liked by search engines.

Those contests which are having many Facebook votes are shown on top of search results on major search engines so that many people could participate in them. When people are making searches on search engines then they can get the related contests on the basis of their searches.

Those people who are using facebook are able to see those contests in top of the list of contests which are having more Facebook votes. With an increase in Facebook votes the credibility and demand of the contest is increased. If you have a contest on facebook then you must try to get many Facebook votes so that the importance of your contest could be increased.

This process could be completed by using many ways. There are free and paid modes for getting Facebook votes for any type of contests. When you are posting your contests and paying attention on getting more and more Facebook votes then you are on your way to have more online exposure.

This will be helpful in many ways and you are able to attract the attention of many people. You can post links of your sites on your contest pages on facebook and have more exposure. Facebook votes would be increased and many people will check the contests and links which will be helpful in more online exposure.

Many people are using facebook in routine life as it is the best social site from all over the world. Therefore it is good to have contests on facebook and more Facebook votes so that you could use the traffic on your site or links of your choice. If you have many friends and followers on facebook then you are able to use free modes for increasing Facebook votes for your contests.

If you are willing to try exchanges then you must locate the exchange which is having many members so that you can get many Facebook votes for free. You can also invest some money in order to start the process of getting more and more Facebook votes for your contests.

Any method can be used and you will be getting more and more Facebook votes. Make sure that your contests are providing complete details for users so that you can use Facebook votes for having a lot of traffic on the site and also on the linked sites through your contests.

You can post many contests from time to time and get Facebook votes for them in order to have more exposure on internet. When you have many Facebook votes for your contests then you will get traffic automatically from search engines and also from facebook.

High quality Facebook votes

Facebook votes must be of a high quality in order to get a lot of traffic and exposure from real users. If you are purchasing Facebook votes then these are not of a high quality as these are in the form of fake accounts which will cast votes for your contests in order to increase the numbers.

When the number of Facebook votes is increased for your contests then you are able to attract Facebook votes which are of a high quality. It means that fake Facebook votes could be used for getting Facebook votes of a high quality.

If you are asking your friends to cast votes on your contests in facebook then you are able to get high quality Facebook votes but the amount would be less as compared with Facebook votes which you can purchase. Quality is the main difference in case of Facebook votes which are obtained through free and paid methods.

If you are participating in communities on facebook and asking them for casting Facebook votes then you are able to get high quality Facebook votes. When you have used paid methods for increasing Facebook votes then more people will think that your contest is good and they will also participate in it.

This will give you more Facebook votes which are of a high quality. It is hard to get high quality Facebook votes in start as the contest will be new and you must be in need of some methods for increasing Facebook votes.

You can use some investment in order to increase the number of Facebook votes in start. When you are having many Facebook votes then you are able to get high quality

Facebook votes from real humans. These Facebook votes will increase the worth of your contests and you will see much traffic from contests.

You must make sure that you are using professional presentation for your contests. Those contests which are not made in a professional manner are not going to get a lot of engagement from users and more Facebook votes will also not work as much. If your contests are made in a professional manner and giving useful information then engagement will be increased and you will get more traffic.

Facebook votes could be increased through different methods. You can choose the methods of your choice and have more Facebook votes which will attract more people to participate in your contests. When you have done the initial working for getting Facebook votes for your contests then you are on your way for getting more and more traffic.

This will give you high quality Facebook votes from internet and many users of facebook will become engaged with your contests. A good start is required for making the process of getting high quality Facebook votes automatic.

Once you have a good start then you are on your way for getting more and more Facebook votes which will increase the worth of your contest. While making investment you must make sure that you need high quality Facebook votes in order to have more importance for your contests.

Free modes of getting Facebook votes

Facebook votes are important and these could be obtained by suing free modes. You can ask different people on facebook so that they can give you Facebook votes on your contests.

Votes on facebook are counted as importance of post. If your contest is liked by many people then you will see that many Facebook votes are received in a short time period. It is important to have some marketing for your contests so that you could get Facebook votes.

Many contests are launching on facebook from time to time so it is not possible to have your contests getting attention without any efforts. You have to spread the details about your contests on facebook so that users of facebook could get information and provide you Facebook votes.

If you have many friends on facebook then you can ask them for getting Facebook votes. You can spread the voice about your contests in communities in facebook so that many people could give you Facebook votes and check details.

You must make sure that you are discussing the contests on facebook on relevant places. These methods are free but there are no guarantees that you will get Facebook votes as per needs. Many people will check your contest but all will not cast their votes.

Some people will leave the contest without casting votes and some will try to cast the vote but will not complete the process so the vote will not be counted. This free mode is giving instant results but results are not guaranteed as many people will not take the requests seriously for casting Facebook votes as per your needs.

Many people are using free modes and there are some successes as well but complete success is not obtained. Those people who have many friends and followers on facebook could get good results through sending messages to their friends and followers.

Many of their friends and followers will check the contests and cast their votes. All the accounts on facebook are not so popular so they cannot get desired votes through requests. First of all you must work on increasing the number of friends in your facebook profile.

You can post good contents and also participate in contests of others so that many people check your profile on facebook and get in your followers list. When you have many friends and followers on facebook then you can post the contests and ask for getting Facebook votes.

This will give you many votes and this process will work for free. If you are willing to get instant results then there are many paid services which can be used. You are required to invest some money and professionals will give you desired number of votes in your budget.

There are many packages on internet which are helpful for getting votes. You can make selection of the desired packages and get Facebook votes in the required time. Many professionals are giving votes from facebook profiles which are looking real and increasing the worth of your contests.

Factors affecting Facebook votes

Facebook votes are dependent on many factors. First of all you must have good quality contests in which people will like to have engagement. When you have launched the contests in facebook then you must try to get Facebook votes from people.

You can share links of your contests on different sites so that people could come and check the contests. You can also share links of your contests with many users of facebook for free. Many of your friends will be checking and casting Facebook votes on your contests.

You can use exchanges in order to increase the number of Facebook votes for your contests. Some money could be invested for purchasing Facebook votes for any type of contest. This method is fast and you will see increase in the number of Facebook votes in a short time period.

You can use credit system in exchanges in order to get more Facebook votes for your contests. This process will be used for more online exposure and marketing for your contests. Trends on facebook are changing with time so many factors are related with contests for getting more and more Facebook votes.

You must not stop the process of marketing your contests so that more Facebook votes could be attracted from time to time. In start your contest will be checked by users and if it is made in a professional manner then your contest will get more engagement. You must include useful information in your contest which will be liked by users.

Buying some Facebook votes for the contest is also a good thing in order to attract more real humans for casting Facebook votes. If you have many followers and friends in facebook then your contests are going to get more exposure. You can share links of your contests with your followers and get Facebook votes easily.

Many followers are ready to check the posts and you will see instant increase in traffic to your contests. However it is not guaranteed that all the followers will cast their vote for your contest.

In order to have guaranteed increase in Facebook votes for any type of contest you must make some investment. Professionals are available on internet through which you can get guaranteed increase in the number of Facebook votes for your contests.

These professionals have unique IP addresses which can be used for getting votes for contests. You can increase Facebook votes through these services for making the contest more important. When the number of Facebook votes is increased through paid methods then your contest will be checked by many visitors regularly so that they could also cast a vote.

There are social exchanges which are used for getting Facebook votes for contests. Some participation in those exchanges is required so that users could get credits for free and use them for getting Facebook votes.

You can use paid modes in these exchanges for getting fast Facebook votes for desired contests. You can use other sites which are giving paid Facebook votes for contests. These are some factors which can be used for increasing the number of Facebook votes.

Facebook votes for online exposure

Contests on facebook could be used for online exposure if they have many Facebook votes. Many people are posting contests on facebook regularly in order to have a lot of traffic for free. It is important to work on contests on facebook so that more traffic could be obtained.

Online exposure could be obtained by using Facebook votes on contests. It is important to have many Facebook votes for online exposure as launching a contest is not enough for getting traffic and benefits. You must use some ways to increase Facebook votes on your contests and you will get more online exposure which will give you more traffic.

You must post the contents on your contest with care so that people could participate in them and cast their votes. You can also use the traffic on your contests on facebook for getting traffic on other sites. Many sites could be linked with your contests with many Facebook votes.

When the number of Facebook votes is increased then you can have benefits in the form of traffic on all the linked sites. Online exposure could be obtained by using Facebook votes on contests. Many people are using Facebook votes and increasing them for their contests so that they can have more exposure on internet.

Those contests which have many Facebook votes are going to attract more and more traffic and give more and more online exposure. Many contests on facebook are launched in order to get online exposure. Many people think that launching the contests is enough for getting online exposure without working on getting Facebook votes.

This is not the case as Facebook votes will be required for increasing the worth of contests on facebook. With more Facebook votes for any contest you are on your way for getting more traffic and more exposure.

Many Facebook votes are considered by search engines as the particular contest is liked and used by users from all over the world. In this manner the search engines are showing that contest for people looking for related topics in searches. This will give traffic from search engines and many more people will participate for giving Facebook votes.

In start you must use some methods for getting Facebook votes for your contests. When you have started the process of getting Facebook votes then your contest will be important and famous so that you could get more and more exposure. Online exposure through contests on Facebook votes is high in demand as it is giving benefits in the form of more traffic which is of a high quality and more chances of sales.

If you are willing to save time then you must invest some money for getting Facebook votes for your contests. If you have some time then you can use free modes for increasing Facebook votes for your contests.

Any method could work and you are able to get benefits for more exposure through your contests. You can search for the desired methods on internet and apply to get them for having more Facebook votes for your contests and more online exposure.

Attraction through Facebook votes

Facebook votes are helpful for attraction of visitors to contests so that they can cast votes for more benefits. Those contests which are having more Facebook votes could attract more visitors and get more exposure.

People on facebook are thinking that a particular contest is very important therefore it is given many Facebook votes. It you are willing to get attraction for your contests through Facebook votes then you can invest some money.

You can purchase Facebook votes from professionals and include them for your contests. This process is simple and you will get the desired number of Facebook votes in your contests in the set time period. This process is fast and there are no problems in using it for increasing Facebook votes as the contests will get many more numbers in the form of Facebook votes.

Those contests which have good first impressions are going to get more attraction. Those first impressions could be built by increasing Facebook votes. More people are attracted towards contests in facebook which have more Facebook votes.

Paid methods for increasing Facebook votes are used for getting attraction. This method is available through many sites and professionals are ready to give Facebook votes for contests on payment of some money.

You can attract many real humans towards your contests when you have many Facebook votes. These Facebook votes could be purchased in some time period through professionals.

This process is fast and you will be able to have more attraction of your contests when you have many Facebook votes. Many search engines are giving importance to Facebook votes and those contests which are having many Facebook votes are shown on higher in search results.

You can get on top of search results for specific keywords if you have contests in facebook with many Facebook votes. In this manner Facebook votes could be helpful in search engine optimization.

It is not easy to get Facebook votes so search engines are considering them useful and showing the relevant contests for users. This will show the contests with many Facebook votes for users and traffic from search engines will also be increased. You can also show your contests on top of search results if you have many Facebook votes.

You can attract more and more people to your contests when you have got many Facebook votes. This process of attraction will continue and you are able to have more votes for more attraction and exposure. Demand of facebook is increasing with time and many people are using this social site in routine life.

Contests in facebook are checked by many people on a regular basis and those contests which are having more Facebook votes are getting more attraction and engagement from users. It is not enough to launch a contest and leave it so that it could grow and get Facebook votes automatically.

You have to work on your contests on facebook for getting Facebook votes so that you can have benefits. You can increase attraction for your contests on facebook when you are increasing Facebook votes by using free and paid modes.

Facebook is a social site which is used by many people in routine life. Votes on facebook are obtained in different ways. You can post any type of content on your account and get shares and likes for it. These are types of votes for your posted contents.

Those posts which are showing many likes and shares are viral and liked by many people. There are many people who are providing fake likes and shares for increasing number for posts.

There are also pages on facebook which have fake likes and shares. This is to impress others so that they can come and join the page. If a page is having thousands of followers and likes then new users will be attracted to like and share the contents.

Fake likes are used for increasing interest and attraction of real humans so that they can like and share the contents. Main thing is to get real followers as they will give benefits in the form of shares and likes. Contests on facebook are posted in different niches.

There are many people who are posting contests on facebook in order to increase attraction. People on facebook are willing to take part in contests so that they can share their knowledge and thoughts with a chance of getting prizes as winners. Different types of contests are posts on facebook and posters are inviting people to cast votes.

When a good prize as a return is offered against any contest on facebook then the chances of getting more votes are increase. Those contests which are liked by users are showing a lot of activity in the form of votes and shares.

If any contest is having many votes then it will be shown on top of list of contests. It means that the people looking for certain contests will be shown that contests on top and help them in engagement.

Search engines are also showing contests in search results. These are the contests which are liked and shared by people on internet. Many people are using facebook and taking part in contests. You can post many types of contests in facebook in your niches in order to get engagement.

When you have many contests on facebook which are getting engagement then you can post links on them of your choice. In this manner you are able to post links which are related with your blogs and sites. You can post affiliate links related with the niches of contests on facebook and get instant results in the form of more traffic.

When traffic on your links is increased then it will give more chances of getting sales. If you are looking to get a lot of exposure on facebook then you can post contests and insert links. These links will be helpful in driving the traffic back to your site. You can promote your contests in facebook in order to have more exposure and more chances of getting traffic to your linked sites.

With more links to your site you are able to have more traffic through search engines. Contests on facebook are high in demand because these are providing a lot of engagement and traffic from people from all over the world.

Facebook is used by many people in routine life and they are looking for participation in contests. Many types of contests are launched on facebook from time to time in order to get engagement and participation from users. You can encourage people to cast votes in contests through different means.

You can give notifications about your contests to people in order to get traffic to your contests. When more people will come to your contests on facebook then a lot of them will participate and cast votes. You can increase the process of getting more votes by spreading links for your contest pages on different sites.

Facebook is a good site and many people are using it therefore your contests are going to have a lot of exposure but when you are sharing the links on other sites then more exposure and more engagement is obtained. There are many good sites on internet which are giving important products and services but these are not promoted in a right manner.

Without promotion it is hard for any site to show up on search engines and get any traffic. Traffic of visitors is important for any site for getting success. Facebook is a social site which is used by many people and links of your site on facebook are helpful in delivering traffic and chances of conversions. You can post contests on facebook and then see results in the form of participation and engagement from people.

Your links of your blog or site of other affiliate links on your contest pages are also helpful in getting traffic when you are getting good results for your contest. When your contest is successful then you are able to get many votes for your contest.

People like to share the contests which are providing useful information and presented in a professional manner. Make sure that your contest is professional and liked by people so that you can have more engagement and traffic to the linked sites.